I0797766

JAWS
OF FLORIDA'S BEACHES

Published by Arcadia Children's Books
A Division of Arcadia Publishing, Inc.
Charleston, SC
www.arcadiapublishing.com



Manufactured in the United States

Designed by Jessica Nevins
Images used courtesy of Shutterstock.com; vi RichartPhotos/Shutterstock.com; p. 6 JennLShoots/Shutterstock.com.

ISBN: 9781467196222
Library of Congress Control Number: 2026930629

# JAWS OF FLORIDA'S BEACHES

by Sarah Fabiny

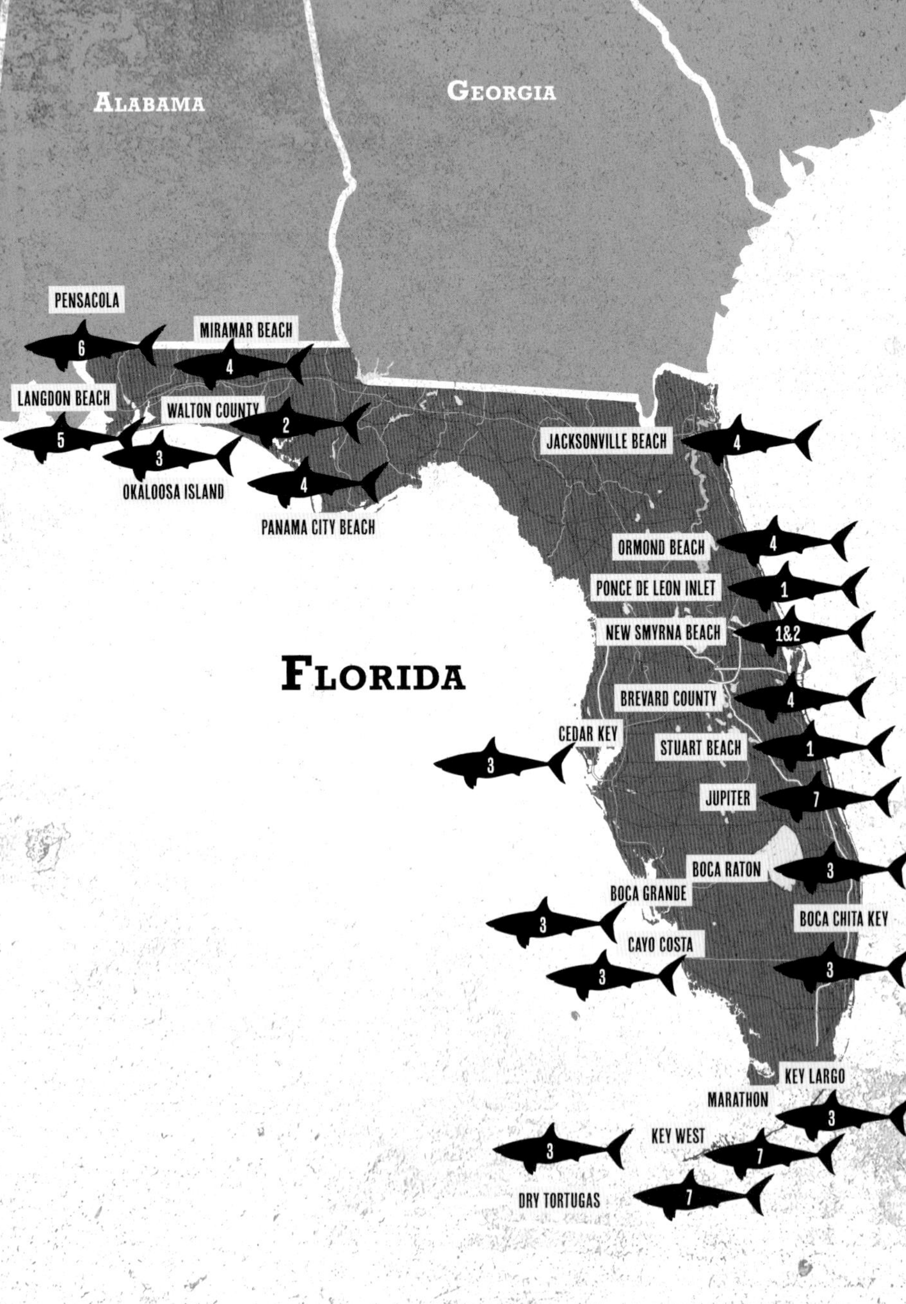
Alabama
Georgia
Florida
PENSACOLA
6
MIRAMAR BEACH
4
LANGDON BEACH
5
WALTON COUNTY
2
3
OKALOOSA ISLAND
4
PANAMA CITY BEACH
JACKSONVILLE BEACH
4
ORMOND BEACH
4
PONCE DE LEON INLET
1
NEW SMYRNA BEACH
1&2
BREVARD COUNTY
4
CEDAR KEY
3
STUART BEACH
1
JUPITER
7
BOCA RATON
3
BOCA GRANDE
3
BOCA CHITA KEY
CAYO COSTA
3
3
KEY LARGO
MARATHON
3
KEY WEST
7
3
DRY TORTUGAS
7

# Table of Contents & Map Key

Universal Studios Theme Park, Florida

# INTRODUCTION

Every year, over 140 million people from around the world head to Florida to visit the theme parks, explore the national parks, and soak up the sun on the beautiful sandy beaches. Perhaps you're one of them! If so, you probably have great memories of the time you spent in the Sunshine State.

So, did you take a big GULP when you saw the title of this book? But since you've picked it up and taken a look inside, you must be a bit curious about the sharks that make their home in the waters along the Florida coast. Because not only do tourists flock to Florida every year—so do sharks. We are frightened, but also fascinated, by these creatures that have been on the planet for more than 400 million years. We can't wait for *Shark Week*, we celebrate the 50th anniversary of the movie *Jaws*, we dress up as sharks for Halloween, and we even got a song about a baby shark on the pop music charts!

It's easy to understand why sharks frighten us. They are extremely successful predators of the sea, have multiple rows of razor-sharp teeth (that regrow when they fall out!), and may sometimes bite swimmers and surfers. But these encounters are incredibly rare. Across the world, fewer than one hundred people are attacked by sharks each year, while in the same time period, over one hundred *million* sharks are killed by humans.

However, the more we learn about sharks, the more we understand just what incredible creatures they are. For instance, did you know that sharks have been on our planet since before the age of dinosaurs? Or that they have a "sixth sense" called electroreception, which helps them detect electrical fields in the water? Can you believe some species of shark live for over 400 years? And some species even glow in dark.

If you're starting to think twice about going back in the water the next time you're in Florida, of course you should keep your eyes and ears open and be safe. After all, nearly every body of water in the Sunshine State is home to wild animals like alligators, sharks, and snapping turtles—so it's important to be aware of your surroundings anytime you swim or wade. Still, it's unlikely you'll encounter or even see a shark while you're in the ocean. You're more likely to be struck by lightning or get extra recess for the entire school year than you are to be bitten by a shark—the chances are about one in 11.5 million. And sharks are not the vicious, deadly monsters you may have seen in movies or on TV. In real life, they are more interested in fish and seals than they are in humans. In fact, most shark attacks usually occur due to "mistaken identity" because a shark thinks a splashing human is a fish or a seal.

That said, shark encounters *can* be pretty scary, and this book shares some of those true (and truly terrifying!) stories. But it's important to remember that these incidents are rare, and sharks have far more to fear from us than we do from them. In *Jaws of Florida's Beaches,* you'll learn all about the kinds of sharks that swim in Florida's waters, and what complex and mysterious creatures sharks really are. You'll also discover how scientists track shark attacks in Florida and around the world, and how they use this information to better understand these amazing animals. And by the end—believe it or not—you might just see sharks and their behavior in a whole new way.

New Smyrna Beach
Volusia County, Florida

# SHARK BITE CAPITAL OF THE WORLD

Do you love spending a day at the beach? You can relax in a beach chair, soak up the sun, and read a book. You can play a game of beach volleyball, paddleball, or Frisbee. Or you can go for a swim in the surf. Florida is the perfect place for those activities because it has over 8,000 miles of coastline. It has more coastline than any state, besides Alaska and Hawaii. Not all those miles of coastline are accessible or open to the public, but nevertheless, Florida has a lot of beaches! And if you go for a dip, you'll be sharing the water with a variety of sea creatures—including sharks.

While sharks live in the water along Florida's coastline, it doesn't necessarily mean that swimming at a Florida beach is dangerous. Every state along the East and West Coasts and the Gulf of Mexico has reported shark attacks (except for New Hampshire). But it is worth knowing that of all those states, Florida takes the number one spot for shark bites. And within Florida? That title goes to Volusia County. Volusia County is north of Orlando and south of Jacksonville, and includes the cities of Daytona, Ormand Beach, and New Smyrna Beach—which has earned the nickname "shark bite capital of the world."

An agency that keeps track of shark attacks around the world reports that between 1882 and 2023, there were 351 unprovoked shark attacks in Volusia County. (An unprovoked shark attack is when a shark bites a person in the ocean without the person doing anything to bother or tease it.) That's more than double the number of attacks recorded by Brevard County, which holds the number two spot for shark attacks in Florida.

One of the earliest recorded shark attacks in Volusia County was fatal and is believed to have occurred around 1902. The victim was a postal worker canoeing in Ponce de Leon Inlet, when the current swept his canoe out and capsized it. His body was found several days later with his limbs missing, likely bitten off by sharks. Fortunately, fatal shark attacks are very rare. The last one reported in Florida was in 2010, when

a shark killed thirty-eight-year-old kiteboarder Stephen Schafer about a quarter mile offshore near Stuart Beach in Martin County. More recent shark attacks have been instances of a shark clamping down on a person's arm or leg, likely due to mistaken identity.

In 2024, four people encountered sharks in just one week along the shores of Volusia County. A shark bit one man at New Smyrna Beach on July 4. The following day, a shark attacked another person in the same area. On July 8, a shark bit a fourteen-year-old taking part in lifeguard training just several miles up the coast at Ponce Inlet. And on July 10, a shark bit a Missouri teenager on vacation. Shockingly, some occurred in only knee-deep water—a reminder that sharks sometimes follow schools of baitfish into the shallows.

In July 2025, Matt Bender from Winter Park, Florida, had a frightening encounter with a shark while surfing at New Smyrna Beach. While recovering in a hospital bed, Matt recounted the experience: "Just like a lightning strike—the shark came out of nowhere. I just felt it chomp down on my arm. It felt like a bear trap." Matt said that the shark shredded his arm, but it "immediately let go, and it was gone in a flash." At the time of the attack, Matt was in just five feet of water.

Matt quickly tied his surfboard leash around his arm as a tourniquet to stop the bleeding, before managing to paddle back toward the shore. His cries for help attracted a man and his daughter, who helped him onto the beach. Lifeguards and paramedics treated Matt until an ambulance arrived to transport him to the hospital in Daytona Beach. Despite the close call, Matt reported that he was determined to get back to surfing. He said that encountering sharks on Florida's coast "comes with the territory."

Not long after Matt Bender was attacked, eighteen-year-old surf instructor Sam Hollis came face-to-face with a shark at New Smyrna Beach. Sam was teaching a surf class when a big wave crashed over him. He climbed back on his board and let his feet dangle off the back of it. Sam said that the shark "just grabbed me by my foot and yanked me off my board." Even though the shark took him completely by surprise, Sam knew he had to fight back. He kicked the shark hard enough to knock it away, then swam to safety. At the hospital, doctors treated Sam for multiple bite wounds on his foot. Like Matt, Sam said he knows the risks of surfing at New

Smyrna Beach and would be back in the water as soon as he recovered.

There are several reasons why shark encounters occur more often in Florida. The biggest one? Sharks love Florida for the same reasons humans do: the miles of shoreline and relatively warm waters all year long. Some sharks that live off the Florida coast stay in these waters permanently, while others migrate here every year for the plentiful prey that also loves the comfortable temperatures of the ocean.

Many spots along Florida's coast, including New Smyrna Beach, have sandbars and currents that trap fish. These areas are popular with surfers and swimmers, but they're also a perfect feeding ground for sharks. Many shark bites are actually accidental "tastes" instead of an intentional attack, as a shark may have mistaken a person's foot or hand for a fish. This is more common when the water is murky, which is why you should avoid swimming after storms when it's harder to see what's around you—and harder for sharks to tell you're not a fish!

Even though sharks have very good eyesight in clear water, they're also sensitive to contrast and movement, which can trigger their hunting instincts. Shiny jewelry or brightly colored swimsuits and wetsuits might catch a shark's attention. And if a swimmer or surfer is splashing, a shark may assume it's a fish and go check it out.

Florida accounts for close to half the total shark attacks in the United States each year, but

chances are, you won't encounter a shark while enjoying the sun, sand, and surf in the Sunshine State. Still, it's important to remember that any time you step into the ocean, you are playing in a shark's backyard, so be respectful and stay aware of your surroundings. Swim smart—and never swim alone!

# SPRING BREAK SHARKS

Spring break! It's that time of year in March or April when thousands of people flock to Florida. Families come to enjoy a week or two off from work and school. College students hit the beaches to let off steam and have some fun before or after their midterm exams. And some folks head south just to escape the very last bits of winter back home. But whatever your reason for visiting the Sunshine State during spring break, you're sure to have lots of company! It's estimated that each year, more than 1.5 million people head to Florida during spring break season. All those crowds splashing around in shiny jewelry and brightly colored swimsuits

and wetsuits can attract sharks swimming in Florida's coastal waters.

The concept of spring break in Florida started almost one hundred years ago. In the mid-1930s, a college swimming coach from upstate New York took his team to Fort Lauderdale so they could use a new Olympic-sized pool for some

early training. Other swim team coaches quickly caught on, keen to give their swimmers a head start on practicing for competition season. It wasn't long before heading to Florida in the early spring became an annual tradition for swim teams looking for a warm, sunny place to train.

Throughout the 1940s and 1950s, word spread beyond swim teams, and more college students discovered this sunny southern beach destination. By 1953, around 15,000 students were traveling to Fort Lauderdale every spring. In 1959, *Time* magazine mentioned spring break in an article, and in 1960, the movie *Where the Boys Are* was released. The movie followed four college women during their spring break in Fort Lauderdale, and it was a smash hit. Suddenly, even more college students wanted a bit of sand, sea, and surf. They flocked to places like

Daytona Beach and Miami Beach as well as Fort Lauderdale. By 1985, it was estimated that 370,000 students visited Fort Lauderdale for spring break, and in 1986, MTV launched its first Spring Break Special.

In 2005, Hollywood decided to mix the fun of spring break with the fear of shark attacks. That year, a made-for-TV movie called *Spring Break Shark Attack* hit people's screens. It tells the story of a young woman who travels to Florida to join her friends for spring break. A marine biologist, who happens to be the young woman's older brother, is investigating a reef where sea turtles have been found dead and some swimmers have recently disappeared. It turns out that a pack of deadly tiger sharks has arrived in the area and is preying on the turtles and the unsuspecting swimmers. He races to warn the spring breakers, including his sister, before they all fall prey to the sharks.

Now we know why people travel to Florida for spring break, but why are the sharks there? Some shark species live in Florida's waters year-round, while others are just passing through as they migrate. Sharks are sensitive to water temperature, and they move to stay within their preferred range. As summer approaches,

many sharks migrate through Florida's coastal waters—some heading north along the Atlantic coast as temperatures warm, while others move to breeding grounds in the Gulf of Mexico where female sharks give birth in the summer. It turns out a lot of these sharks are cruising by Florida just as tourists arrive for spring break. More sharks in the water plus more people in the water equals more shark encounters.

In April 2001, a two-mile stretch of New Smyrna Beach closed to swimmers and surfers after sharks bit three people on the same day. At least seven people were bitten by sharks in the area that week. Patrol officers suspected that the large schools of baitfish swimming close to shore attracted hungry sharks, which likely mistook the hands and feet of swimmers and surfers for fish. All the injuries were considered minor, but

Richard Lloyd, a twenty-two-year-old surfer, needed surgery to repair damage to his left foot. He said the shark came at him "out of the blue, totally unexpected, not even a chance. . . . I didn't see anything, no fish around—just bam!" Rob Horster, the Volusia County Beach Patrol captain at the time, reminded swimmers and surfers, "That's their turf. You're going into their home."

In March 2013, a huge shiver of sharks (yes, that's really what a group of sharks is called!) migrating north shut down beaches along Florida's eastern coast and kept lots of spring breakers out of the water. Researchers at Florida Atlantic University in Boca Raton counted more than 15,000 sharks in the area. Most of them were less than 200 yards from shore.

Tourists weren't the only ones headed to the beach during spring break in 2025. A record-breaking great white shark named Contender was also hanging around the waters off the Florida coast in March of that year. It's estimated that he weighed 1,600 pounds and was nearly fourteen feet long. (That's about as long as a full-size SUV!) Contender stayed a good distance from shore, thankfully, but researchers made sure to keep an eye on him. By October 2025, Contender had made his way to the Gulf of St. Lawrence off the Labrador Peninsula in Canada.

If you visit Florida for spring break, chances are you won't encounter or even see a shark. But it's worth following these safety rules: only swim in areas with lifeguards on duty, don't enter the water if sharks are known to be present, get out of the water immediately if sharks are sighted, and never harass a shark.

# SHARKS FOUND ALONG FLORIDA'S BEACHES

There are over 500 species of shark in the world. The waters around Florida are home to about fifty of those species, with fifteen being the most common. The most commonly encountered sharks in the waters off Florida are the bull shark, lemon shark, and sandbar shark. Other species seen in Florida include the blacktip shark, nurse shark, and tiger shark. So, let's meet them!

## BULL SHARK STATS

| | |
|---|---|
| Length: | 7 to 11 feet, but can be up to 13 feet |
| Weight: | 200 to 500 pounds |
| Coloring: | gray upper body, white belly |
| Diet: | crustacean, seabirds, turtles, rays, dolphins, smaller sharks |
| Status: | near threatened |

Bull sharks are responsible for more unprovoked attacks in Florida waters than any other species, making them the Sunshine State's most dangerous shark (just like great whites in California and Australia). Bull sharks have a stocky build with a thick head and body that tapers down to a wide, powerful tail fin. This species is known for being territorial and aggressive, especially when protecting its space. Bull sharks have a unique osmotic system, a special ability to regulate salt in their bodies, which allows them to survive in both saltwater and freshwater. Because of this, they can swim into many of Florida's freshwater rivers and canals—places you might not expect to find a shark—and are especially common in Florida's shallow coastal waters.

In 2022, seventeen-year-old Addison Bethea was scalloping in shallow water off Keaton Beach in Cedar Key when a nine-foot shark, suspected to be a bull shark, suddenly clamped onto her leg. Her brother Rhett, a firefighter, raced into the water and fought off the shark by punching it repeatedly while Addison poked at its eyes. Rhett pulled his sister onto a boat, applied a tourniquet to stop the bleeding, and rushed her to the hospital. Addison later had to have her leg amputated, but she remained in good spirits and said she would return to the water once she healed. Her story reminds us that even though scary incidents like this can happen, shark encounters remain incredibly rare—and most Floridians continue to safely enjoy their beaches and waters every single day. But when dangerous encounters do occur, bull sharks are often the species involved.

In June 2025, a nine-year-old girl in Boca Grande had a terrifying encounter with a bull shark. While snorkeling, the shark bit her hand, almost severing it at the wrist. In Walton County in June 2024, three attacks occurred on the same afternoon, prompting authorities to close a twenty-five mile stretch of beach. One of the victims had to have her arm amputated. Authorities suspect an eight-foot bull shark was responsible for the attacks.

## LEMON SHARK STATS

| | |
|---|---|
| Length: | 8 to 11 feet |
| Weight: | 200 to 400 pounds |
| Coloring: | yellowish-gray upper body, white belly |
| Diet: | crabs, crayfish, bony fish such as mullet and catfish |
| Status: | near threatened |

Lemon sharks get their name from the yellow coloring on their upper body. This coloring

camouflages the young sharks as they mature. This species lives in the shallow waters around mangroves until they are about twelve years old, and their yellow color helps them blend in with the sandy seabed. Researchers have trained lemon sharks to swim through different colored doors to find food, suggesting that they have strong color vision. Tests have indicated that the eyes of a lemon shark are up to ten times more sensitive to light than a human's eyes, which means they may be able to see starlight.

Lemon sharks rarely bite humans, and there are no recorded fatal lemon shark attacks. However, even though these sharks don't pose a strong threat, attacks have occurred when people get too close. In August 2025, a lemon shark bit a man who was trying to take a photo with another lemon shark that had been caught off the coast of Cayo Costa, a popular destination for boating, fishing, and shell collecting. In February 2022, a six-foot long lemon shark bit a woman on the foot while she was snorkeling near the Dry Tortugas islands. She defended herself by punching the shark several times, and it swam away.

## SANDBAR SHARK STATS

| | |
|---|---|
| Length: | 6 to 8 feet |
| Weight: | 100 to 200 pounds |
| Coloring: | brownish-gray upper body, white belly |
| Diet: | bony fish, octopuses, squid, eels, skates, rays, shrimp, and crabs |
| Status: | endangered |

True to their name, sandbar sharks prefer sandy or muddy areas along the Florida coast. They often swim in bays, harbors, and the mouths of rivers. You can recognize them by their tall dorsal fin on their back, short round snout, and large, broad pectoral fins. Sandbar sharks usually swim in groups, and their bodies are build for power and speed.

Sandbar sharks are closely related to bull sharks, but they are not as aggressive as their shark cousins. Since they prefer smaller prey and tend to avoid beaches and the surface, sandbar sharks pose little threat to surfers and swimmers. Even though sandbar shark attacks are rare, their size does make them a potential danger. However, there have been no recent reports of sandbar shark attacks along Florida's beaches.

## BLACKTIP SHARK STATS

| | |
|---|---|
| Length: | 5 to 6 feet, but can be up to 8 feet |
| Weight: | around 40 pounds, but can be up to 200 pounds |
| Coloring: | dark gray to brown upper body, white belly, black-tipped fins |
| Diet: | bony fish, skates, rays, squid, and crustaceans |
| Status: | near threatened |

Blacktip sharks prefer shallower water and are usually found in coral reefs, bays, sandy flats, mangrove swamps, and estuaries. They are rarely seen in deep water. Blacktip sharks are quick and energetic, and they have been seen making spinning leaps out of the water while chasing schools of small fish. They usually travel and hunt in groups.

Because blacktip sharks like shallow water, they often swim where people are swimming and surfing. Though they are usually timid and keep their distance from humans, they sometimes show curiosity toward swimmers, surfers, and divers. Blacktip sharks may become aggressive when prey is nearby, and attacks have occurred when a shark mistakes someone's arm or leg for a fish. Blacktip sharks have been involved in about sixteen percent of shark attacks around Florida, but most of these incidents result in only minor wounds. In September 2025, a blacktip shark bit an eight-year-old boy while he was snorkeling off Key Largo. Although he had injuries to his knee and shoulder, he made a full recovery.

## NURSE SHARK STATS

| | |
|---|---|
| Length: | 7 to 8 feet, but can be up to 13 feet |
| Weight: | around 200 pounds, but can be up to 500 pounds |
| Coloring: | blend of gray and brown |
| Diet: | shellfish, crabs, lobsters, squid, stingrays, and small fish |
| Status: | vulnerable |

Nurse sharks are one of the world's more unique species of shark, and are also considered one of the gentlest. It's not clear where this shark got its name, but it may come from a very old word, *nusse*, which translates to "cat shark." This likely refers to the sensory organs that hang from a nurse shark's chin, resembling cat whiskers. Nurse sharks have a flat, wide head and a long, flexible tail fin that can be up to nearly one-fourth its total length. These sharks are bottom dwellers and spend much of their time in caves, crevices, and reefs. Most species of shark need to keep swimming to stay alive because they must keep water moving through their gills. However, nurse sharks use muscles in their mouth and cheeks to pump water across their gills, allowing them to rest peacefully on the ocean floor.

Unprovoked nurse shark attacks in Florida are extremely rare, and none have been deadly. Most nurse shark bites happen because people have bothered or provoked them. In 2016, a woman swimming in Boca Raton learned this the hard way when a two-foot-long nurse shark bit her arm and wouldn't let go. Witnesses said that the woman and her group had been taunting the shark and holding it by its tail before it bit her. The woman had to be transported to the hospital with the shark still attached to her arm!

## TIGER SHARK STATS

| | |
|---|---|
| Length: | 10 to 14 feet |
| Weight: | 850 to 1,400 pounds |
| Coloring: | gray to blue-green upper body, white or yellowish belly, dark, vertical stripes or spots on their sides, which fade as they age |
| Diet: | fish, rays, seabirds, dolphins, seals, turtles, and other sharks |
| Status: | near threatened |

The tiger shark is considered the second most dangerous shark to humans, after the great white shark. (Though bull sharks are not far behind.) Tiger sharks can be found out in the open sea, but they also make their way to murky coastal waters such as harbors, inlets, lagoons, and estuaries. Despite being large and slow-moving, tiger sharks are highly effective predators that ambush their prey with short bursts of speed. And they aren't particularly picky eaters—they are nicknamed the "garbage can of the sea" because they'll eat just about anything, including tires, plastic buckets, and old furniture they find floating in the ocean. They tend to hunt alone, but researchers have observed them socializing with each other, especially in shallower waters.

Every summer since 2021, tiger sharks have congregated around a pier at Okaloosa Island, between Fort Walton Beach and Destin. It started with a group of about ten tiger sharks, but each summer the number of sharks increases, even reaching over one hundred sharks. Scientists believe the sharks are drawn to the thousands of small fish that die around the pier due to a lack of oxygen in the crowded water. (In other words, an all-you-can-eat buffet for the sharks!)

Along with great white and bull sharks, tiger sharks account for some of the deadliest attacks around the world. In Florida, tiger shark encounters are relatively rare. However, when they happen, the injuries can be severe—or even fatal. In 1981, a twenty-six-year-old man named Mark Meeker tried to swim three miles across Tampa Bay on a bet, but a large shark, most likely a tiger or a bull shark, bit him during the swim. He died from his injuries, becoming the second person that year to die from a shark bite in Florida. More recently, in October 2025, a suspected tiger shark bit a man snorkeling off the coast of Boca Chita Key in Biscayne Bay. The man was hospitalized but recovered from his injury.

Now that you've met some of the sharks that spend time in Florida's waters, we hope this is as close as you get to any of them!

# SHARKS 101

Sharks are among the oldest creatures on our planet. Some scientists believe that the earliest shark-like fish appeared on Earth over 400 million years ago. That's about the same time that trees appeared. Dinosaurs did not start roaming the planet until about 230 million years ago—meaning sharks had already been swimming in the oceans for over 170 million years before dinosaurs even existed. With all that history, sharks definitely deserve our respect!

A shark's skeleton is made of cartilage, not bone. (Cartilage is an elastic tissue. In a human body it is found in the joints, ears, and nose.) Because of this, shark skeletons don't turn into fossils easily, so scientists have had to rely on finding shark teeth to learn about prehistoric sharks. Fortunately, shark teeth are hard, and sharks continuously lose and regrow teeth throughout their lives. This is why shark teeth are some of the most common fossils found.

Ancient sharks looked different from their modern-day relatives. The biggest difference? On modern sharks, the upper snout is longer than the lower jaw; on ancient sharks, they were

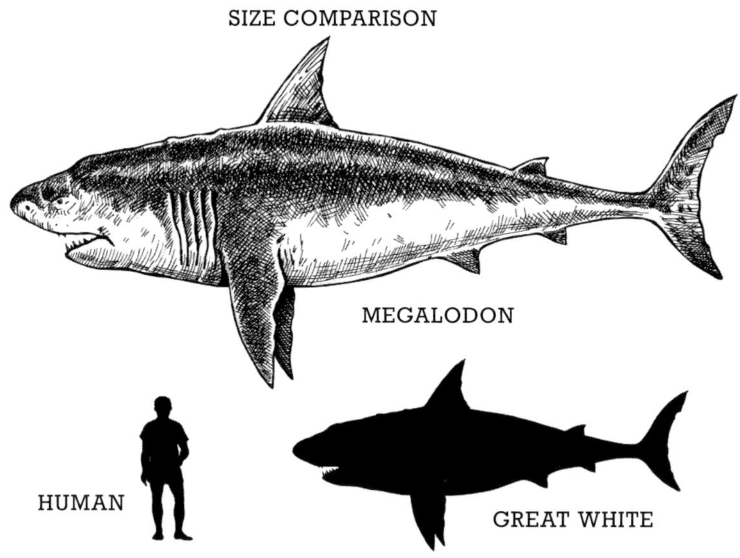


the same length. A few million years ago, a massive shark called megalodon ruled the oceans. (If you've seen *The Meg* movies, you know about megalodons.) Megalodons are believed to have been up to eighty feet long—that's the length of a volleyball court. A fully grown megalodon may have weighed as much as 188,000 pounds—about the weight of *nineteen* African elephants!

While the massive megalodons are now

extinct, smaller modern-day sharks can still be extremely dangerous. It's believed an eight-foot bull shark that probably weighed several hundred pounds attacked and killed Jamie Daigle off Miramar Beach in June 2005. Jamie and a friend were swimming a couple hundred yards offshore when the shark, feeding on a school of fish, struck. A surfer named Tim Dicus heard Jamie scream and saw her friend frantically swimming toward the shore. When Tim reached Jamie, she was face down in bloody water. He saw that the shark was circling back to strike again, so he pulled her onto his surfboard. As Tim paddled himself and Jamie toward shore, the shark followed them. Two other swimmers came out with a raft and helped bring Jamie onto the beach. She was rushed to the hospital, but sadly, she was pronounced dead upon arrival.

Modern-day sharks come in all shapes and sizes. The smallest shark species is the dwarf lantern shark, which is only eight inches long and can fit in the palm of your hand. The largest shark species is the whale shark. It grows up to sixty feet long, which is the length of a lane at a bowling alley. Goblin sharks can be bright pink, and hammerhead sharks have heads shaped like—you guessed it!—hammers. There's even a cookie cutter shark, which gets its name from the perfectly round, cookie-shaped bites it takes out of its prey. However, despite their size, color, or shape, most species of shark are sleek, and their bodies are made for swimming fast.

One quick and streamlined shark, believed to be either a bull or tiger shark, caused the death of Richard Clark Best, Jr. in 1934. He is one of the youngest recorded victims of a fatal shark attack in Florida history, and it remains Brevard County's only deadly shark attack on record. Richard was standing in chest-deep water when he suddenly called out to his father that something had bitten him. Richard's father carried his son to the beach and discovered that Richard had a large bite wound on his hip. The boy was taken to the hospital, but he died from extreme blood loss and shock.

What makes sharks such powerful predators? Sharks have extremely powerful jaws, and their teeth are razor-sharp A shark can have between fifty and 300 teeth, which are arranged in multiple rows. New teeth are constantly growing behind the older ones in the front, and the new teeth replace the ones that are worn down or lost. During the course of its life, a shark can go through tens of thousands of teeth!

However, even with all those teeth, sharks can't actually chew their food. When they catch their prey, they shake it to tear off chunks, which go straight to a shark's stomach to be digested. A shark's digestion is slow, so it doesn't necessarily need to eat every day.

Sadly, a shark's powerful jaws proved deadly for James Neal in 1959. The twenty-six year-old U.S. Army lieutenant and five other divers were spearfishing off the coast of Panama City. When the divers met up at the end of their excursion, they realized James was missing. Divers in the area began searching for him, and one reported

seeing a blue shark and a mako shark. James's diving equipment was discovered the next day, several hundred yards from his last known location, but his body was never found.

Besides their powerful jaws, sharks have other features that make them excellent hunters. A shark's skin is covered in millions of tiny, toothlike scales called dermal denticles. These scales are made from the same material as human teeth: enamel and dentine. They provide protection from parasites and predators, and also reduce drag for more efficient swimming. The scales point toward a shark's tail, so if you rub a shark from head to tail, it feels smooth, but if you rub from tail to head, it feels rough, like sandpaper.

Although it might not be obvious by looking at them, sharks have pretty amazing eyesight and a fantastic sense of smell. Scientists estimate that a shark's eyesight is about ten times better than a human's in clear water. They also have a layer of reflective cells in their eyes that helps them see extremely well in the dark. (Cats have these cells as well—it's what makes their eyes glow in the dark when you shine a light on them.) A shark's eyes are also good at detecting movement in the ocean. And because a shark's eyes are positioned on opposite sides of its head, it has a nearly 360-degree field of vision. However, sharks have two blind spots: directly in front of the snout and right behind the head.

In 1976, a shark might have spotted Ricky and Michael Karras, young brothers from Tennessee, as they swam near the Jacksonville Beach Fishing Club, close to a pier where fishermen regularly caught sharks. The boys disappeared, and it was assumed they drowned. However, Michael's body washed ashore with shark bites to his shoulder and leg, believed to be from a bull or hammerhead shark. Ricky's body was never found. This was the first deadly shark attack in Florida in fourteen years; it hadn't recorded a fatal attack since 1962.

A shark's sense of smell is even more impressive than its eyesight. Up to two-thirds of a shark's brain is dedicated to smell, and sharks are sometimes called "swimming noses" because their sense of smell is so powerful. They use their nostrils, called nares, to detect tiny amounts of chemicals in the water. As water flows into their nares, special cells send signals to their brain, helping the shark identify what it's smelling. Sharks use ocean currents to help them follow a scent, similar to how a dog follows a smell on a breeze. When a shark identifies a scent trail, it swims in a zigzag pattern. This keeps it in the "smell lane" and helps it to get closer to its prey. Some shark species can sniff out the blood of prey from incredible distances—one part of blood to one million parts of water. That's equal to one teaspoon of blood in an Olympic-sized swimming pool!

That powerful sense of smell may have led sharks to Christy Wapniarski, her boyfriend, and another couple in the water after their boat capsized in rough seas off the coast of Ormond Beach in 1981. The two couples didn't have life jackets, and they clung to the hull overnight. In the morning, they decided to swim to shore. While they were swimming, Christy called out to her boyfriend, "Swim to me! I think I'm going to die!" She was the weakest swimmer, and her boyfriend assumed she was drowning. But Christy had been attacked by a shark. When her boyfriend reached her, she was very badly injured and had no pulse. Christy's boyfriend and another member of their party tried to swim Christy back to shore, but they made the difficult decision to leave her behind when they realized she was dead. Incredibly, after eight hours of swimming, Christy's boyfriend and the other couple made it back to shore. Christy's body was never found.

Many shark species are apex predators. An apex predator is an animal at the very top of the food chain with no natural predators once it is full-grown. Although orcas and sperm whales sometimes hunt sharks, human beings are their greatest threat. Sharks kill about five to ten people worldwide each year, but fishing, habitat destruction, pollution, and climate change kill an estimated 100 million sharks annually. Because of this, many shark species are endangered, and about one-third of all shark species risk extinction.

Other factors that make sharks vulnerable include producing only a few young, growing slowly, and having long lifespans. This makes it difficult for shark populations to bounce back once their numbers decline. However, several organizations around the world are working to protect sharks through education and research, establishing protected marine areas and enforcing sustainable fishing practices. Sharks are an important part of the ocean ecosystem, and we need to protect them so they can continue swimming in the seas for millions of years to come.

# 2001: SUMMER OF THE SHARK

In July 2001, moviegoers were flocking to theaters to see *Shrek*, clubbers were dancing to Usher's "U Remind Me," fans of *Friends* were waiting for Season 8 to hit their TV screens, and people in Florida were afraid to go into the water. In fact, people on both the East and West

Coasts of the United States didn't want to wade into the ocean. It was the Summer of the Shark.

The Summer of the Shark began July 4th weekend. It made newspaper headlines, TV news, radio broadcasts, and even the cover of *Time* magazine. The story was all over the news until September 11, when the world then turned its attention to the terrorist attacks on the World Trade Center.

On July 6, eight-year-old Jessie Arbogast was standing in shallow water at Langdon Beach, off the coast of Pensacola, when a six and a half-foot bull shark attacked him. The shark bit off Jessie's arm and severely injured his thigh. While a bystander pulled Jessie out of the surf, Jessie's uncle ran into the water, grabbed the shark by the tail, and dragged it onto the beach. As Jessie was being airlifted to the hospital, a park ranger shot the shark and pried open its jaws, retrieving Jessie's arm from the shark's mouth. Jessie's arm was packed in ice and rushed to the hospital, where surgeons miraculously reattached it.

This dramatic incident made headlines in Florida, across the country, and even around the world. Suddenly, the world's attention was on shark attacks. And when a surfer was bitten by a shark on July 15, just six miles from where Jessie had been attacked, the world's attention became laser-focused. Later that month, a fourteen-foot shark believed to be a great white, repeatedly smashed into a charter boat off the coast of Chatham, Massachusetts. No one was hurt, but for about ten minutes, the tourists were terrified as the shark thrashed and banged the boat with its head and tail. When *Time* magazine published its July issue, the cover was a photo of an enormous shark rising out of the water, with the headline, "Summer of the Shark." If people weren't aware of the shark attacks before, they were now! Beachgoers everywhere were too frightened to wade into the oceans.

On August 4, a man from New York was attacked by a shark while on vacation in Freeport, Grand Bahama Island. (Grand Bahama Island is about eighty-five miles east of West Palm Beach, Florida.) He was swimming in about four feet of water just twenty feet from the shore when a shark bit him on the left leg. The man was able to fight off the shark by punching it, and lifeguards dragged him onto the beach. He was then airlifted to a hospital in Miami, where doctors amputated his left leg above the knee. Not long after that attack, a shark bit man who was snorkeling with his wife off Grand Bahama Island.

Many TV networks repeatedly broadcast video clips of a large shiver of sharks off the southwest coast of Florida. This shiver was most likely part of an annual migration, but people began to think that the Florida coast was being hit by a "shark epidemic."

With summer almost over and Labor Day approaching, people hoped that the "Summer of the Shark" was over. But tragically, that wasn't the case. On September 2, at Sandridge Beach in Virginia, ten-year-old David Peltier and his father were in about four feet of water near a sandbar about fifty yards offshore at 6 p.m. David was swimming and his father was on a surfboard nearby. The shark bit down on David's leg, severing the main artery in his thigh. David's father wrestled with the shark and punched it until it released his son. Lifeguards treated David on the beach until paramedics arrived to take him to the hospital. Doctors did what they could, but David had lost a large amount of blood, and he died several hours later.

Shockingly—the very next day—another fatal shark attack occurred, this time in North Carolina. A couple visiting Cape Hatteras with friends were swimming together near a sandbar about twenty feet from shore. All of a sudden, their friends heard them both screaming. Bystanders and their friends raced into the water and pulled the couple to shore. The man had suffered serious injuries to his lower body and had lost a lot of blood; his heart had also stopped. Sadly, he died on the beach before first responders arrived. The woman, who had lost a finger and her left foot, was rushed to the hospital and survived, though she needed months of surgery and rehabilitation.

It felt like the "Summer of the Shark" might become the "Fall of the Shark." However, just eight days later, on September 11, two jets struck the World Trade Center in New York City, and the world turned its attention to this unbelievable tragedy.

Despite the media frenzy around the "Summer of the Shark," you might be surprised to learn that 2001 wasn't an especially dangerous year for shark encounters. When scientists and researchers analyzed the number of shark attacks that occurred worldwide in 2001, they found it was lower than the previous year—seventy-six in 2001 versus eighty-five in 2000. And although sharks killed five people in 2001, they had killed twelve people in 2000. Many people believe that 2001 was a slow news summer, so when the first dramatic shark attack happened, it gave reporters something to focus on. What became the story of the summer that year might not have received so much attention in another year. The "Summer of the Shark" shows how nonstop news coverage can spread fear and make sharks seem like deadly monsters, even though your odds of encountering one remain incredibly low. And as you've learned in this book, sharks deserve our respect and protection—not our fear.

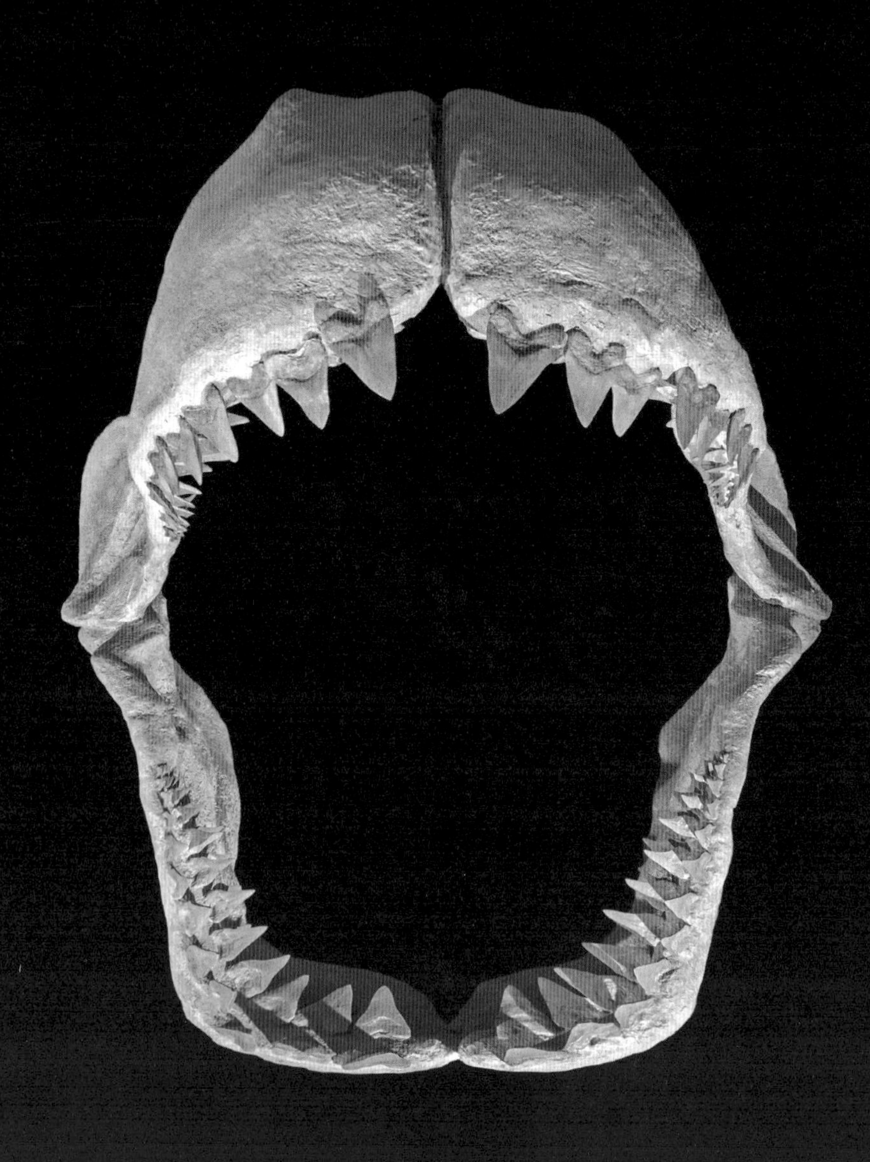

# INTERNATIONAL SHARK ATTACK FILE

Every year, there are about seventy to one hundred unprovoked shark attacks (both fatal and nonfatal) around the world, and on average, about twenty of those occur in the waters surrounding Florida. So, who keeps track of all these encounters? The International Shark Attack File, that's who! It is a database that captures all the reported shark attacks on every continent and in every body of water.

On July 30, 1945, a Japanese submarine torpedoed the USS *Indianapolis* in the Pacific Ocean between Guam and the Philippines, and it sank in just twelve minutes. Of the 1,196 crew members, about 900 survived the initial sinking. These men floated in the open ocean with almost no supplies for four days and nights. Many of the sailors died from dehydration and exposure to the sea and sun. However, it's estimated that sharks killed up to 150 men. The sailors' splashing and the scent of blood in the water attracted numerous sharks, including oceanic whitetip sharks—a species the famous French explorer and oceanographer Jacques Cousteau once described as "the most dangerous of all sharks."

On August 2, an airplane spotted the men, and rescuers pulled them from the water. Only 316 of the 900 sailors who had survived the torpedoing made it out alive, and four more died later in the hospital. To this day, the event is considered the worst shark attack in history. The tragedy revealed that the Navy lacked knowledge about shark attacks and wasn't prepared for situations like this. Determined to prevent a similar disaster from ever happening again, the Navy started researching shark behavior and how to protect U.S. servicemen and women from shark attacks.

So, in June 1958, the Office of Naval Research formed the Shark Research Panel. The Office of Naval Research (ONR) is part of the Department of the Navy. It supports scientific research to ensure the strength and safety of the Navy and the Marine Corps. The Shark Research Panel consisted of thirty-four scientists who were shark experts. They focused on creating an effective shark repellent, studying shark behavior, and tracking shark attacks worldwide.

The National Museum of Natural History at the Smithsonian Institution in Washington, DC, initially kept the database of these shark attacks. In 1968, the Mote Marine Laboratory in Sarasota, Florida, took it over. In the 1980s, the National Underwater Accident Data Center at the University of Rhode Island acquired the database. In 1988, the Florida Museum of

Natural History at the University of Florida in Gainesville became its home—and that is where it remains today.

The database is now known as the International Shark Attack File (ISAF). The Navy ended its support of the database in 1968, but it is now supported by the American Elasmobranch Society, an international organization that studies sharks, rays, skates, and chimaeras (say kie-meer-ruhz). The people who work at the ISAF investigate every reported shark attack around the world, and they also look to fill in gaps in the information from 1968-1988.

Currently, the database has information on over 6,800 shark attacks, dating from the 1500s to present day. Scientists from around the globe volunteer their time to submit this information to the ISAF. They serve as regional observers and pass on data they have gathered about shark attacks in their areas. Because of their work, the ISAF has large amounts of information about attacks, especially in Australia, California, Florida, Hawaii, and South Africa.

Although the ISAF depends on its regional observers to send information, it also accepts reports from the public. The organization then researches and verifies this information. The entire database is available to qualified researchers, scientists, and physicians. Since the database contains sensitive things such as doctors' reports, autopsies, photographs, and victim interviews, the ISAF wants to ensure that the information they hold is only used for appropriate projects.

The earliest recorded shark attack in the ISAF database is from 1580. A sailor, who was part of a crew sailing from Portugal to India, fell overboard during a storm. The report states that the man's shipmates threw him a line to grab hold of, and they pulled him toward the ship. As they did this, "a large monster" suddenly leaped out of the water and "tore him to pieces" before the crew's eyes.

A shark attack that occurred in 1749 later became the subject of a very famous painting: "Watson and the Shark" by John Singleton Copley. Brook Watson, a fourteen-year-old British cabin boy, was swimming in the harbor while his ship was docked in Havana, Cuba, when a shark suddenly attacked him. The shark backed off and then attacked him again. Fortunately, Watson's crewmates pulled him out of the water. Although he lost a leg in the attack, he survived and went on to become the mayor of London.

The first recorded shark attack in Florida occurred near Pensacola in September 1845. A man named Nickerson was fishing when a shark bit him. The shark is believed to have been a tiger shark, and sadly, the man did not survive. Just four years later, in 1849, the first recorded attack on multiple people took place in Florida, also off the coast of Pensacola. Two women, one called Mrs. Cracton, were swimming in the ocean when a shark attacked. The shark seized Mrs. Cracton and pulled her out into deeper water. A man saw what happened and raced to save the other woman. He went back to try and rescue Mrs. Cracton, but disappeared into the water. Mrs. Cracton's body, which was horribly mutilated, later drifted ashore. The man's body was never recovered, but some of his clothing washed up on the beach, and people assumed a shark had killed him as well.

The ISAF's summary for 2024 might be considered encouraging reading for anyone who enjoys a dip in the ocean. It was a pretty quiet year for shark bites. Worldwide in 2024, there were only forty-seven unprovoked attacks, down from sixty-nine in 2023. Of those forty-seven attacks, twenty-nine occurred in the United States—down from thirty-six the year before. Fourteen of the twenty-nine U.S. attacks were reported in Florida. In 2023, Florida recorded sixteen unprovoked attacks, with more than half of them taking place in Volusia County. Why did the number of shark attacks decrease?

Researchers and scientists say factors like fewer people in the water, fewer sharks in certain areas, and improved shark safety awareness, but the exact reasons are still being studied.

Even though you may never gain access to the ISAF database, you can track sharks as they make their way through the world's oceans. The OCEARCH global shark tracker is an online tool that allows you to follow—in real-time!—the

movements of sharks and other marine animals that OCEARCH has tagged. Each tagged animal has a profile with information about its size, story, and migration patterns. You can track everything from green sea turtles in the Pacific and great white sharks in the Indian Ocean, to bull sharks off the coast of Australia and tiger sharks off the coast of Florida. With it, you can start your very own shark file!

# SWIMMING WITH SHARKS

While most people who visit Florida each year want to avoid an encounter with a shark, some people visit the Sunshine State because they actually *want* to meet a shark—or sharks!—up close and personal. These brave adventurers cage-swim or free-swim with sharks in the waters off the coast of Florida.

Cage-swimming is snorkeling or underwater diving inside a protective cage designed to prevent sharks from making contact with anyone inside the cage. It allows snorkelers and divers to come face-to-face with some of the world's most ferocious and formidable predators.

Shark cages were first developed by Jacques Cousteau, who introduced millions of people to the world under the sea through his movies and TV program. He used a shark cage to observe, study, and film underwater creatures,

including sharks. But after the release of the movie *Jaws* in 1975, cage-swimming started to gain popularity. The summer blockbuster about a great white shark that terrorizes a small seaside town fueled a worldwide fascination with sharks, and cage-diving quickly became something that marine biologists, as well as adventure-seekers, were keen to do.

In Florida, from Pensacola to Jacksonville, a number of companies organize cage-swimming or shark diving tours. Depending on the time of year, cage-swimmers in Florida may see tiger, bull, sandbar, and lemon sharks, as well as great hammerhead, dusky, silky, and reef sharks. That's a lot of sharks! A boat takes the brave cage-swimmers and the cage a couple of miles offshore. Usually the cages are large enough to hold around four to six snorkelers or divers, and everyone has enough room to move and observe the sharks. Most of the time, the cage is lowered into the water so that it's just below the surface, not more than ten to fifteen feet. This puts the cage swimmers where sharks spend a lot of their time, and allows them to return to the surface easily and quickly if they need to.

More experienced divers may go down in a cage that holds only one or two people at a time, and they may go down thirty or forty feet. This gives them the opportunity to spend more time underwater with the sharks and see species that hang out in deeper waters. Those brave enough to free-swim with sharks head into the water with snorkels or scuba gear, without the protection of a cage.

There have been no reported shark attacks during cage-swimming activities in Florida.

However, incidents have happened in other parts of the world. In South Africa in 2015, a great white shark bit through the bars of a cage, but miraculously, the tourist inside escaped uninjured. In 2016, off the coast of Mexico, a shark lunged for bait in a tourist's hand and broke into the cage. Luckily, the diver escaped without any injuries.

Although cage- and free-swimming have become very popular with tourists, many people are against it. They argue that this kind of activity disrupts sharks' natural behavior and gets them accustomed to being around humans. It may also cause sharks to associate humans with food, since some companies that organize the tours use chum, or bait, to attract sharks. Scientists and conservationists also worry that activities like this cause people to see sharks as a tourist attraction, rather than an important and essential part of the ocean ecosystem.

The dangers of feeding sharks became clear in May 2017, when the captain of a shark diving tour boat operating out of Jupiter, Florida, was bitten on the hand during one of his company's shark encounter tours. The bite was so severe that he needed to be airlifted by helicopter to the hospital to have his hand surgically reattached. What makes this incident even more concerning is that two years earlier, a court had convicted this same captain of illegally feeding sharks in Florida waters and fined him $1,500.

Florida banned shark feeding in state waters in 2001 because of concerns that feeding sharks could make them associate humans with food and change their natural behavior. However, it is still legal to feed sharks in federal waters more than three miles offshore, which is where most shark tour companies now operate. Even though shark tour operators often claim their activities are perfectly safe, experts point out that feeding sharks significantly increases the risk of bites. When people feed sharks, the sharks can become bolder and more aggressive, putting both tour participants and anyone else in the water at risk.

Shark feeding isn't just dangerous during organized tours. Spearfishing, which involves hunting fish underwater with a spear or speargun, creates similar risks because the blood

and movement from injured fish naturally attract sharks. In July 2024, an eight-foot bull shark attacked a spearfisherman near Key West after the man had just speared a fish. The shark bit him on the shoulder, chest, and legs, and the man's friend had to fight off the shark by shoving a spear into its mouth. In September 2022, a shark bit another spearfisherman on the arm in Marathon, Florida, while he was returning to his boat with a speared fish. These incidents show that whenever food is involved, whether people are feeding sharks on purpose or naturally attracting them with spearfishing, the risk of shark bites to humans dramatically goes up.

If you are brave enough to meet sharks in person one day, make sure that your family or friends book a tour with a company that puts safety and respect for the environment first.

Choose companies that don't use bait or chum to attract sharks and that follow all state and federal laws. While you definitely want to have the adventure of a lifetime, it's also important to educate yourself about how sharks are an irreplaceable part of the world's seas.

# BIG FISH WITH A BAD RAP

It's easy to see why sharks have a bad reputation. They look prehistoric (because they are!); they have rows and rows of razor-sharp teeth; they are portrayed as vicious killers in books, movies, and TV shows; and whenever a shark bites a human, it becomes a top news story. And of course, millions of people tune in to *Shark Week* on the Discovery Channel every summer. Some of the programs discuss conservation efforts and correcting misinformation about sharks, but many of the shows are filled with gory, close-up shots of shark attacks and gruesome stories about these predators. It's no wonder these amazing creatures are seen as the ultimate bad guys.

Sharks may not be as cute as pandas, as cuddly as kittens, or as playful as baby goats, but they should be revered, not feared. And here are some good reasons why:

Sharks have an impressively long family tree. They have been around for hundreds of millions of years, and it's no small feat to change, evolve, and still swim in the oceans over that incredibly long period of time. It's amazing to think of all the animal species that have appeared and disappeared around the world during that time, but sharks are still swimming in all our planet's oceans.

Humans are much more deadly to sharks than they are to us. Nearly one hundred million sharks are killed each year for their fins and meat. Shark finning is the practice of cutting off a shark's fin, sometimes just for the shark fin soup market, and then discarding the shark's body. Sometimes the shark is still alive when this happens, but throwing it back in the water dooms it since it can't swim without its fins.

Many sharks die when they are accidentally caught in fishing nets. They actually suffocate because they can't keep moving to force water, which contains oxygen, over their gills.

The odds of being bitten by a shark are extremely low. You are much more likely to be attacked by a dog, injured in a hunting accident, or struck by lightning. And the odds of being killed by a shark are even lower. Car and bicycle accidents, falls, firework mishaps, and even the

flu are all more likely to be deadly than a bite from a shark.

Sharks help keep the world's oceans and seas healthy. As apex predators, they help control their prey populations, which helps maintain the balance of marine ecosystems. For example, the presence of sharks in some areas stops other animals from overgrazing the seagrass on the seabed. These seagrass meadows serve as important nurseries for many marine species. Sharks also hunt weak, sick, or old animals, which helps prevent the spread of disease and keeps the gene pool of their prey strong.

Of course, this doesn't mean you should run out and try to make friends with a shark. But it does mean that we should respect sharks and appreciate their past, present, and future on our planet. If you are interested in getting involved in shark conservation, there are organizations and charities that work to educate the public about sharks and ensure they have a future. And mark July 14 on your calendar because that is Shark Appreciation Day. The day was created to dispel the fear and misinformation about sharks and raise awareness about the importance of sharks to the world's oceans.

# BEFORE YOU GO: SAFETY TIPS FOR SWIMMING SMART

Since Florida reports the greatest number of shark bites and attacks each year, and one of its beaches is known as "the shark bite capital of the world," it's important to keep these lifeguard-recommended tips in mind when you hit the beaches in the Sunshine State.

1. Never swim alone.

2. Never swim anywhere without lifeguards.

3. Always follow the lifeguards' instruction. They aren't joking when they tell you to get out of the water. That means there is danger.

4. If you see a fin sticking out of the water, head to shore and tell a lifeguard.

5. Avoid swimming at dawn or dusk, as this is when sharks like to feed.

6. Don't swim where there are schools (large groups) of baitfish. Often, they're being hunted by larger fish, including sharks.

7. If you see a large or unusual fish in the water, get back to shore immediately. Better safe than sorry.

8. Don't wear shiny jewelry, play with shiny objects, or wear brightly colored swimsuits in the water—these may attract sharks.

9. Don't splash or thrash around in the water too much—this also may attract sharks.

10. Never tease or injure a shark—or *any* animal.

11. If you see a sick or injured fish or shark, do not touch it. Report it to an adult.

Remember, these tips aren't meant to scare you away from Florida's incredible beaches—they're meant to help you swim smart so you can enjoy them safely! From the calm, turquoise waters of the Gulf Coast and Florida Keys to the rolling Atlantic waves at New Smyrna Beach, Florida offers some of the most beautiful shorelines in the world.

Whether you're building sandcastles in Destin, searching for seashells (or pirate treasure!) on Sanibel Island, or boogie boarding in Daytona Beach, you can have an amazing time *while* respecting the ocean and the incredible creatures that call it home. So, grab your sunscreen, swim smart, and have fun exploring Florida's beaches!

# BIBLIOGRAPHY

## BOOKS

Klinkenberg, Jeff. *The Shark Attack Files*. Gainesville, Florida: The University of Florida: 2016.

MacCormack, Alex and Rod Green, editors. *The Mammoth Book of Shark Attacks*. London, England: Robinson, 2013.

Sobczak, Charles. *Alligators, Sharks & Panthers: Deadly Encounters with Florida's Top Predator – Man*. Sanibel, Florida: Indigo Press, 2007.

## WEBSITES

ABC News. https://abcnews.go.com/GMA/News/woman-lost-leg-shark-attack-describes-shes-recovered/story?id=101341600

CBS News. https://www.cbsnews.com/miami/news/spearfisherman-bitten-by-shark-near-key-west/

First Coast News. https://www.firstcoastnews.com/article/life/animals/a-history-of-shark-attacks-in-florida-jacksonville-tampa-west-palm-beach-stuart-pensacola-panama-city-fernandina/77-880716c6-d500-4cb5-9f8c-6ae376692873

Florida Museum of Natural History. https://www.floridamuseum.ufl.edu/shark-attacks/

Florida Shark Diving. https://floridasharkdiving.com/

Keys Weekly. https://keysweekly.com/42/breaking-marathon-scuba-diver-bitten-by-shark/

Natural History Museum. https://www.nhm.ac.uk/discover/shark-evolution-a-450-million-year-timeline.html

Spearfishing World. https://spearfishing.world/thread/7494-shark-feeding-diver-bitten-by-shark-west-palm-beach/

Time. https://time.com/archive/6664432/why-cant-we-be-friends/

**Sarah Fabiny** is a former associate publisher and editorial director turned freelance writer and editor. She is the author of over fifty children's books, including seventeen titles in the #1 *New York Times* best-selling *Who Was?* series. She lives in Eau Claire, Wisconsin, and is thankful that her only encounters with sharks have been at aquariums.

Dive into even more books by
Sarah Fabiny!

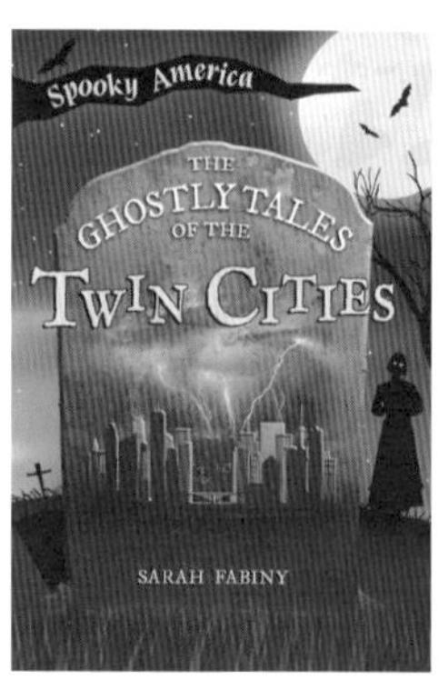


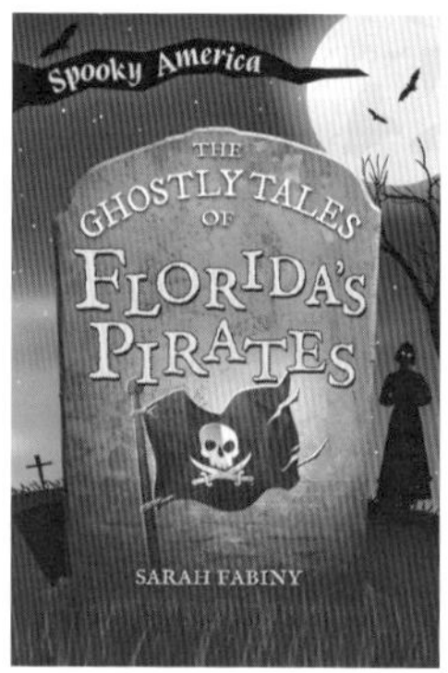